PSYCHO BUSTERS

I

Story by
Yuya Aoki

Manga by
Akinari Nao

Translated and adapted by
Stephen Paul

Lettered by
North Market Street Graphics

Ballantine Books * New York

Psycho Busters volume 1 is a work of fiction. Names, characters, places, and incidents are the products of the author's imagination or are used fictitiously. Any resemblance to actual events, locales, or persons, living or dead, is entirely coincidental.

A Del Rey Trade Paperback Original

Published in the United States by Del Rey Books, an imprint of The Random House Publishing Group, a division of Random House, Inc., New York.

Publication rights arranged through Kodansha Ltd.

First published in Japan in 2006 by Kodansha Ltd., Tokyo.

ISBN 978-0-345-49935-6

Printed in the United States of America

www.delreymanga.com

9 8 7 6 5 4 3 2 1

Translator/adapter: Stephen Paul
Lettering: North Market Street Graphics

Contents

Honorifics Explained

Throughout the Del Rey Manga books, you will find Japanese honorifics left intact in the translations. For those not familiar with how the Japanese use honorifics and, more important, how they differ from American honorifics, we present this brief overview.

Politeness has always been a critical facet of Japanese culture. Ever since the feudal era, when Japan was a highly stratified society, use of honorifics—which can be defined as polite speech that indicates relationship or status—has played an essential role in the Japanese language. When addressing someone in Japanese, an honorific usually takes the form of a suffix attached to one's name (example: "Asuna-san"), is used as a title at the end of one's name, or appears in place of the name itself (example: "Negi-sensei," or simply "Sensei!").

Honorifics can be expressions of respect or endearment. In the context of manga and anime, honorifics give insight into the nature of the relationship between characters. Many English translations leave out these important honorifics, and therefore distort the feel of the original Japanese. Because Japanese honorifics contain nuances that English honorifics lack, it is our policy at Del Rey not to translate them. Here, instead, is a guide to some of the honorifics you may encounter in Del Rey Manga.

-san: This is the most common honorific, and is equivalent to Mr., Miss, Ms., or Mrs. It is the all-purpose honorific and can be used in any situation where politeness is required.

-sama: This is one level higher than "-san" and is used to confer great respect.

-dono: This comes from the word "tono," which means "lord." It is an even higher level than "-sama" and confers utmost respect.

-kun: This suffix is used at the end of boys' names to express familiarity or endearment. It is also sometimes used by men among friends, or when addressing someone younger or of a lower station.

-chan: This is used to express endearment, mostly toward girls. It is also used for little boys, pets, and even among lovers. It gives a sense of childish cuteness.

Bozu: This is an informal way to refer to a boy, similar to the English terms "kid" and "squirt."

Sempai/ Senpai: This title suggests that the addressee is one's senior in a group or organization. It is most often used in a school setting, where underclassmen refer to their upperclassmen as "sempai." It can also be used in the workplace, such as when a newer employee addresses an employee who has seniority in the company.

Kohai: This is the opposite of "sempai" and is used toward underclassmen in school or newcomers in the workplace. It connotes that the addressee is of a lower station.

Sensei: Literally meaning "one who has come before," this title is used for teachers, doctors, or masters of any profession or art.

[blank]: This is usually forgotten in these lists, but it is perhaps the most significant difference between Japanese and English. The lack of honorific means that the speaker has permission to address the person in a very intimate way. Usually, only family, spouses, or very close friends have this kind of permission. Known as *yobisute*, it can be gratifying when someone who has earned the intimacy starts to call one by one's name without an honorific. But when that intimacy hasn't been earned, it can be very insulting.

I
Story by Yuya Aoki
Manga by Akinari Nao

Contents

HUFF
DASH
HUFF
HUFF
There they are, that way!
Swing around, cut 'em off!
Oh no!
This is a dead end! We can't go any farther this way!
Guess we've got no choice but to fight, then!
FWOOOOSH
We can't, Kaito!
Jôi... What should we do?
....
I know what to do.

We'll jump off this cliff.
WHOOOOOOSH
Are you serious?
Yes.
C'mon... No way we can survive a jump from this height.
But Jôi said we should do it, and he would know...
There are fifteen of them.
We'll be surrounded. Got to hurry.
We'll survive.
I guarantee it.

And once we're out safely in one hour and seventeen minutes,

WHOOOOOSH

Look for "Kakeru."

Our future rests on Kakeru.

LEAP

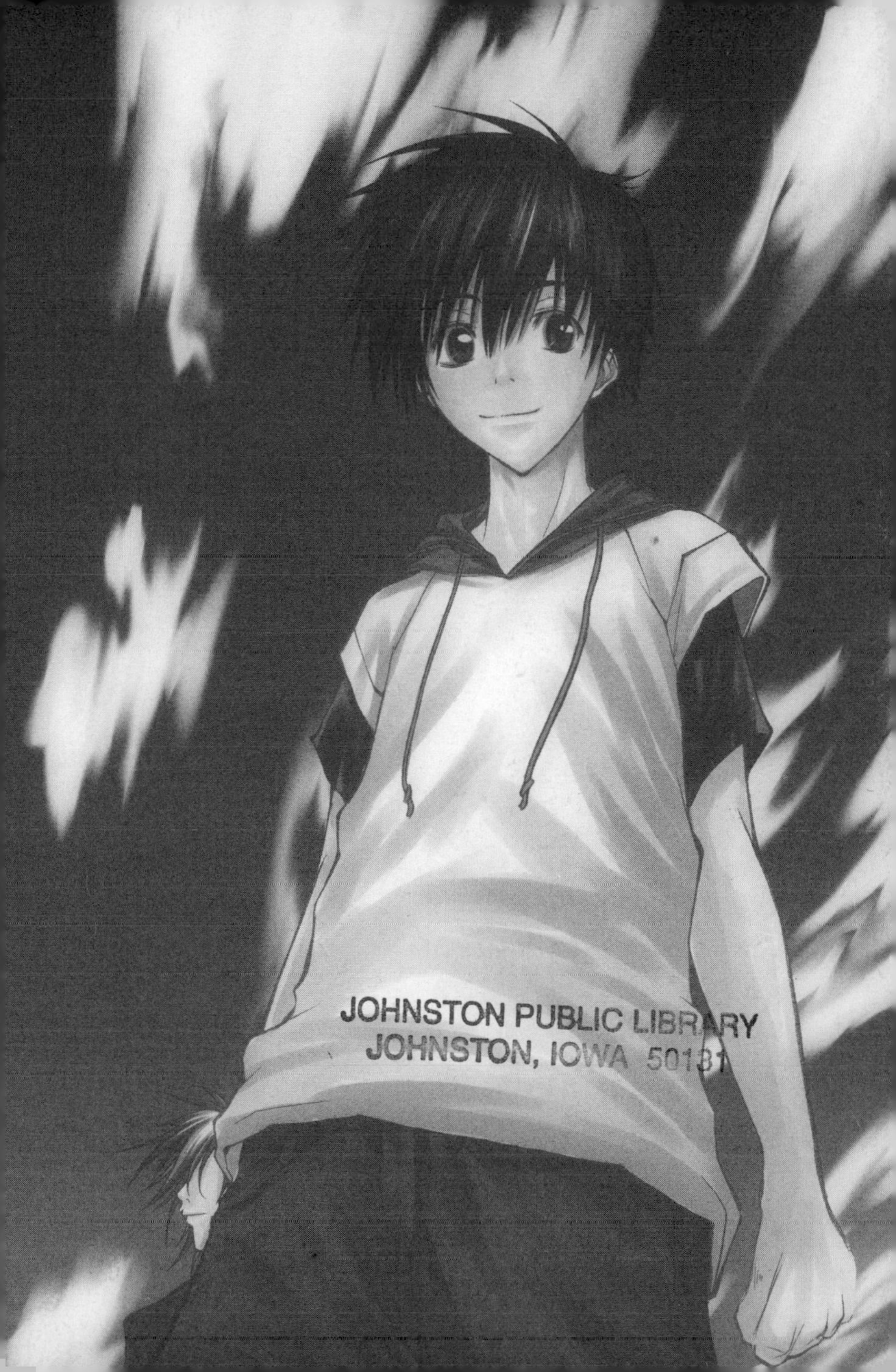

CASE 1 – Kakeru

Psycho Busters

ば~ん
BAM
ど~ん
BOOM
So, how does that look to you?
Well, Kakeru?

Kakeru! I need feedback!
U-Umm... Good... I guess...?
Hey, what else should I bring? I got my passport and swimsuits...
Don't you think we'll want some sunscreen, too?
Good idea!
She's not even listening...
I'm really sorry about all this, Kakeru-chan.
That booking mix-up left us with only three plane tickets.
I was hoping we'd all get to go to Hawaii *together*.

All right, girls, swimsuit hour is over! Get changed!

We're leaving immedi-ately!

Sure thing, Mama.

Good-bye, Kakeru, we're going now.

Don't forget to clean up after yourself.

Sure.

ブオオオー

VROOM

......

Yahoooo!
I'm freeeeee!

No more noisy women.
Dad's out of town, working at some branch office.
And summer vacation starts today.
7 JULY
No one bugging me about my final middle school exams.
I've got a six-day, five-night stretch of solitary, fifteen-year-old freedom...
And I'll make the most of it!

10:00 Living Room

BA-BUMP BA-BUMP

NANAN

12:00 Sisters' Room

6:00 Living Room Again

What should I order?

SPECIAL MENU

Let's see...
I think the tissues are around here somewhere.
There they are.
Prepa-rations com-plete.
Ariel

Living alone is the best!
Ariel

Now if only something totally shocking and exciting would happen, my vacation would be complete.
Too bad that'll never happen.
I mean, the world as I know it...

Is at peace...
MARCH
SCHWIK
Did you find them?
Chief Ikushima, sir!
I'm afraid there's no sign of them...
FWOOOSH
I see.

Do you think it might be time to call this off, Chief...?
...
If they really jumped off this cliff,
They can't possibly still be alive...
FWOOOSH
Do not judge them by your own standards.
I assure you, the four of them are quite alive.
I know this be-cause...

They are not ordinary human beings.

They are "psychics" whose powers surpass all imagining.

Yip yip!
BLAM
BLAM
You may kill them if the situation requires it.

WHOOOSH
LUNGE
Taste the wrath of my legendary blade!
Graaah!
SLASH!

My hero!
A
POP
Princess Ayaka!
Y-Your boob are pressing on me.
ひたっ
SQUEEZE
All is well!
The world has been saved!
The End

カタ
TAP
カタ
TAP

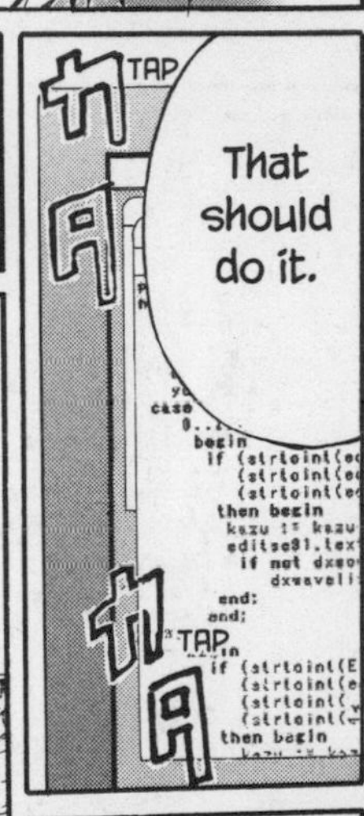
カタ
TAP
That should do it.
カタ
TAP

I'm here at Hachijû-kurihama Beach!
The water is full of people on vacation—
Man, I'm thirsty.

I really wanna finish up this game during vacation!

I bet it's nice at the beach...
I bet it'd be fun with a girl-friend...

THUMP
GRAB
Not that *that'll* ever happen...

There's nothing for a totally boring guy like me to do. I can only find dreams and adventures in computer games.

I've already given up on real life... So games are my escape.
Of course, I know they're not real, but the "extraordinary" I desire in life can be found in games.
KCHAK
See, in a video game, I could just open a door and there would be a girl there, waiting for me...
And in a porno game, she'd be naked.

……

……

You're...

"Kakeru," right...?

……

Ah...

Aaaaaah!

A g-g-ghost!

A translucent girl!

I'm sorry!

WHAM

Whatever it is, I'm sorry!

Please don't put a curse on me!

Dear God, save me!

SLIP
Uh...
N... No, stop...
S... Stay away!
But... wait,
She's kinda cute... I think.
Wha...
SWISH

Whaaaaa?!
SLOOP

Is...
Is
she...
Moving
through
me?!

しーん
SHHH
Huh...?

I'm no hallucination.
Whaaa?! Now she's speaking inside my head?!

......
Noth-ing hap-pened.

Did I just hallucinate that?

I'm being pos-sessed by a ghost!
Trust me, you don't want to possess me!
There's no point to it!
Nooo!
Oh, I know! Where are the *ofuda*?!

クスッ
GIGGLE

Don't worry. Settle down.
I'm... not a ghost.
I'm alive, all right.
Huh...?
Alive?

And I can show you proof. Just follow along.
No! Stop!
Please, make your peace and go to Heaven!

HOP
BOINGGG
Wait. Huh?

LURCH
LURCH
My body's moving on its own...

Stop iiiit!
THUMPA THUMPA THUMPA
Stop meee!
......

HOO
HOO
We're here.
H... Here?
You'll find my body and my friends inside this busted-down house.
W-When you say, your "body," does that mean...

Formerly Pretty Girl
Noooo!

I already explained that to you!
Give it a rest!
Bwaah?!
THWOCK

My friend's hurt and can't move.
Punched by my own fist...
So I need you to save him.

I'm waiting inside, so come on in!
HMPH HMPH
Huh...? Hey, wait...!

She's gone...
I can move again...

Was that all a dream?
Yeowww!
PINNNCH
I guess not...

ビクッ
FLINCH
HOWWWWL!

......

I can't do this...
I'll just go back home.
No use risking my life...

Help us!

But then...
She *did* say her friend needed my help...

And besides, wasn't I always ***hoping*** that something would happen to me?

ZBOOM
Adventure and...

しゅううう
HISSS
Ex... cite... ment...?
Don't do that, Xiao Long!
Kakeru, are you all right?!
Aya-no!
ちっ
Tch!
He's not an enemy, Xiao Long! I brought him here!
What was... that...?
Ouch
He kicked my butt without even touching me...
Oh! Aren't you the—?
The naked ghost chick!
BLUUUSH
Y...You don't have to shout...

I can touch you now...
And you're not see-through. I guess it was true...
POKE POKE
つん つん
Didn't I tell you I wasn't a ghost?
It's a power called "astral projection."
Az-trall pro-jeck-shun?
...What's that?
How do you spell that?
Well, the kanji are "ghost," then "body"...
...So you *are* a *ghost.*
......

Say, why don't I introduce you!
This is Xiao Long. He's one of us.
Huh... So I guess she really *isn't* a ghost.
Oh yeah! Didn't you say someone was hurt?
Is that him?
Oh, right!!
I'll show you to Jôi, but you need to take him to the hospital-
HOP
Jôi?
WHACK
Wait.
What is it, Xiao Long?!

We were caught unawares... The enemy's already surrounded us.
I'd say about ten of them.

S-Sur-rounded by... enemies?
What's that mean...?

They're probably all equipped with firearms.
You mean guns?!

Are you guys, like, on the run?! Why?!
Don't worry, Kakeru. Just settle down.

B-But the guns are real, right?!
If you get shot, you'll still die!
Who the heck are they?
Terrorists? Or are they...
"Farmers."
Farmers?
Cultivators.
They are called Farmers because they harvest us like crops.

Farmers... Harvest...?

Wh... What do you mean...?

But my specialty is "fixing."
Not so good at "breaking." Can't control it so well.

All right.

JUMP

POW
POW POW
POW

FWISH

!!

He's gone! Where'd he go?!

Yi!

BOOM

SHH

DMM

Er!

WHACK
WHACK

San!

Si!

Wu!

W...
Wow!!

Dmmm

CRUNCH

And finally...
オオオ
FWOOO
ゴゴ
GMMM
Shi!

ドガッ
THWUD

ぱんっ
PAT
ぱんっ
PAT
Got them all.
Good work, Xiao Long.

We are...
Psychics.

Psy-chics...?!

Like... ESP?

Yep.

We escaped from a psychic development facility the Farmers run.

My powers are astral projection and telepathy.

Xiao Long is a master of qigong, and can even heal minor injuries.

PEACE
ブイ

W... Wow...

T-Then, what was that trick he used to knock me and those bad guys backward?

That was another use of qigong. As it can heal, so can it destroy.

In that case, why don't I clean out your ears for you?
!!

Ikushima!
You people have been more trouble than you're worth...

A... A pistol?!
A...A... A real one?!

TENSE
......

I wouldn't move, if I were you, Xiao Long.
Unless you don't care what happens to these two.
KCHIK
Grr...

Now where...
Is Jôi?

He must be nearby. Where?
...
...I don't know.
Really.
Is that your final answer?
SHOVE
Aaah! Nooooo!
Make it quick. I'm sure you're aware of my short temper?
Stop it!
He has nothing to do with this!

!!
Oh, really?!
How silly of me.
Of course. Why didn't I realize that earlier?
What...

So I assume we can get rid of him, then?
SHHH
Huh...?

Well, in that case...
N-
No!

BLAM
Good-bye.

What a day.
It's not in my nature to *actually* seek adventure in real life.
I knew I shouldn't have done this.
Come tomorrow, I'm just going to be another unexplained death in a newspaper article.
To think, this is going to be the last moment of the fifteen years I've wasted in life.

Sigh...
Here it comes, flashing before my eyes.
Ariel
Ariel
How lame.
What a crappy life!
I...I don't want it to end this way...

I don't want this!!

POW

Ah...

シュウウウウウ
HISSSSS
Uh... huh?

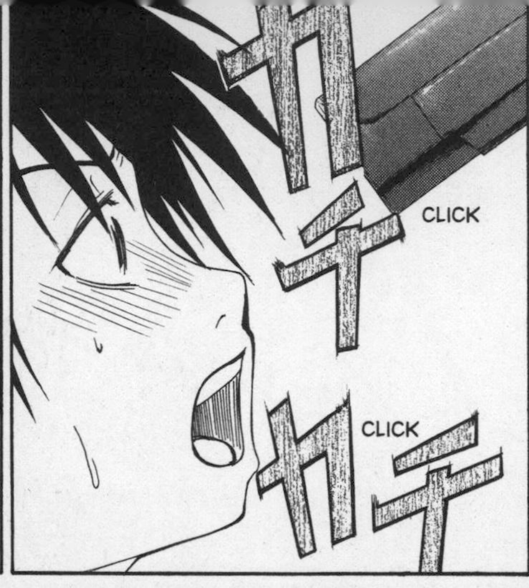

That's it...

CLUNK

This power...

BOOOM

B-BOOOM

The shack collapsed?!
And only above my head...
DOOM
DOOM
DOOM
Retreat!
Damn.
Lucky...
...me?

That's it.

I've found him.

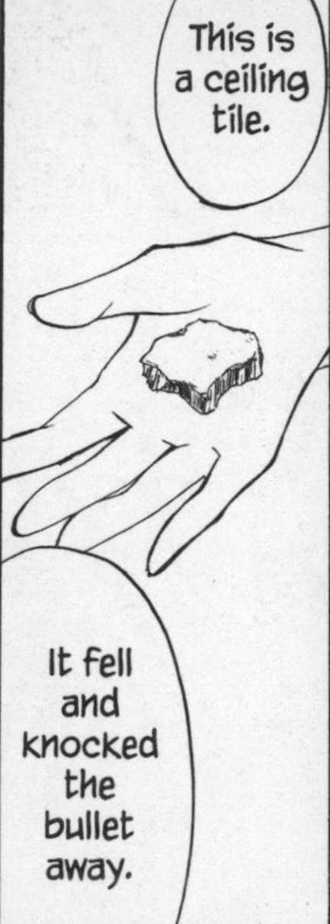

At any rate, we should leave. We can't stay here any longer.

It's too dangerous.

Right. Where's your friend? The one who's hurt.

Right here.

CRACK

This is our leader, Jôi...

REACH
GRAB

Huh...?

Jôi...kun?

It's been a while, Kakeru.
......?
"Been a while"?
W... What is this feeling...?
Why doesn't he feel like a stranger to me...?
Good work, Ayano, Xiao Long.
You kept your promise.
You followed my "words."
Kakeru.
...

Your "story" is just beginning.

You are going to save the world...

...Huh?

CASE 2 – Kaito
Kakeru,
You are going to save the world...
......
...Huh?

TWEET
TWEET
Mmh...
Morning...
Whew.
Talk about a nightmare...
A naked girl shows up out of nowhere, some sinister group tries to kill me,
and then they tell me to "save the world." It was crazy...
SHOVE
You are going to save the world.
After that, I took advantage of my family's absence to let them stay over at my house, and I even slept next to a...
SQUEEZE
Hmm...?

YEEEES!!....

I wish it *had* been a dream...
......
Actually, maybe this isn't so bad...
Muh? Where am I?
I wanna go back to sleep!
んー
Urhhh
A-A-Ayano!

Kakeru, what's wrong...

SHUNK

Xiao Long
Powers: Qigong

No, Xiao Long... It's not what you...

Hmya mya

Pillowww...

......

Come on, Ayano! Wake up! It's time to get up!

ゆっさ

SHAKE

Whew...

ゆっさ

SHAKE

You are *such* a sleepy-head!

Ayano
Powers: Astral Projection

FSHHH
Jôi!
Are you okay?!
Kaito is...
In... Yoko-hama...
SHHH

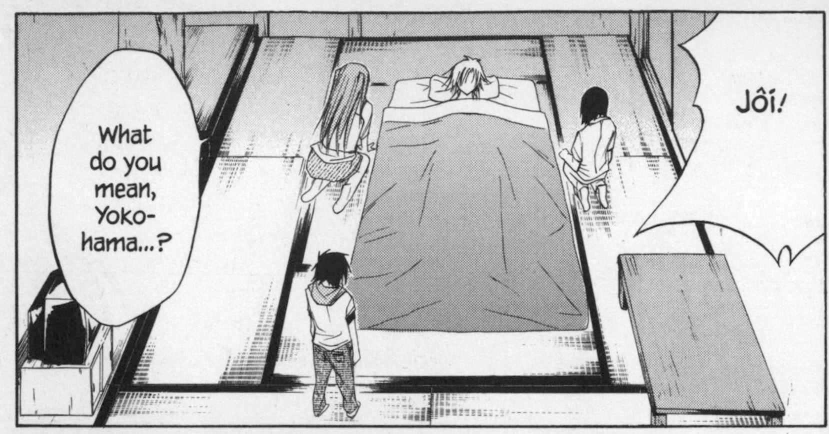
Jôi!
What do you mean, Yoko-hama...?

Who's Kaito?
He's our friend. He escaped with us.
Oh no!
WHOOOOOSH
C'mon... We can't survive a jump from this height.
We jump from here.
LEAP
Our future rests on Kakeru.
Jôi said we would all survive, so it's good to hear he's still okay.

......

So, who are you people, anyway?!
I get that you're psychics and all, but why did you run away?
And these "Farmers" who are chasing after you... What's with them?

I'm sorry, Kakeru.
I can't tell you that until Jôi wakes up.

Just by knowing what you already do, you're in an incredible amount of danger.
If I tell you now, you'll regret it later.
Oh, okay...

This presents a new problem, however.
What's that?
If we go to find Kaito, we'll have to leave Jôi behind.
What if the Farmers attack while no one's here...?
I'll go alone.
You can't!
Then *you'll* be in danger!
We have to move as a pair.
Hmm...
So... What you really need is a safe place to keep Jôi for now?
Yes.
In that case...I know someone who can help us.

This is a school, right?

Yeah. Is that a problem?

Well, is there really anyone we can count on here?

No one's here during vacation...

Ha ha... Well, I don't know if we can count on her, but I'm sure she'll under-stand...

Faculty Room

Huh?!
MOOF
Now here's a familiar face, Kakeru!
How've you been?
Little twerp!
STRUGGLE STRUGGLE
じたばた
S... Stop, that hurts! Hiyama-san!
Oh, come on, it's what I always do, isn't it?
....
Always...?

Awwow me to intwoduce you...
Hiya!
This is Hiyama-san. She works at this school...
Why are you dressed like that, anyways?!
It's hot! I was taking a bath!
Umm...
Oooh, he's so *darling*!
SLAM
Oh? Who's this?
That's Xiao Long.
He's like a precious little doll!
I like this one better!
So... That's where her taste runs...

Psychics, huh...?
I think I get the gist of it. I just don't know what to think.
FWOO
ふぅー
So you believe us?
Hey, you saw it happen, didn't you?
Well... Yeah.
Then who am I to doubt you?
But if you're *really* psychics, then...
Then... what?
....
Bend some spoons for me!
Is she... really trust-worthy...?
あんぐり
SLUMP

Based on your story, I can't just leave the poor kid out in the cold.
SHWICK
Leave it to me, kids! I'll take him under my wing.
...Okay, I'm just kidding.
You will? Really?!
Now we can go to Yokohama!
Yeah!
However. Be careful.

Look at what they're packing.
I can't believe you brought that back with you, Xiao Long...
These people clearly have backing in very high places...
In a worst-case scenario, they could even be involved with the government.
In any number of countries...
You have to be prepared for the conse-quences.

You failed to recapture the psychics?!

This will wreak havoc on the plan...
There is no need to fear.

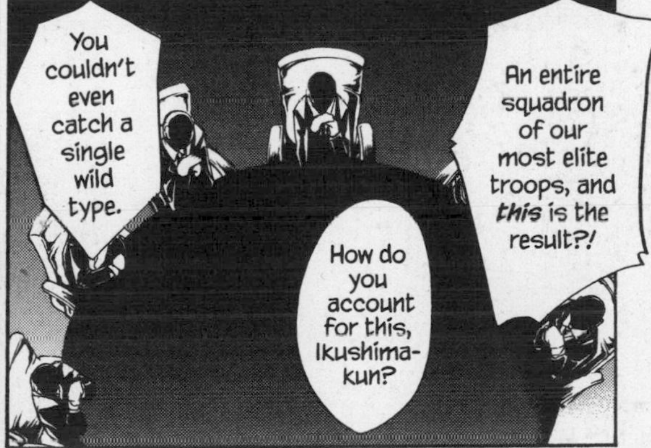
An entire squadron of our most elite troops, and *this* is the result?!
You couldn't even catch a single wild type.
How do you account for this, Ikushima-kun?

I will use the Category Ones.

SLAM
What?!
The three of them should have no problem capturing runaway wild types.
Besides, I already have a very good idea...
SLIP
Of where those wild types are heading.
BEEP
You can expect a rain of blood in Yokohama tomorrow.

I will leave the media manipulation in your hands.
Good day.

So this is Yokohama...
關帝廟道
Some of these restaurants look really good...

Look, Kakeru!
Sigh... What happens if we get attacked again...?
And in the end, here I am, tagging along
Doesn't this peach bun look *delicious*?!
BOOOOM
C'mon, Kakeru, try it out!
Just take a bite!
GYACK
That looks a little suggestive...

. . . .
?
What in the *world* am I thinking?!

Huh?
What's wrong?
All of a sudden...
The neighbor-hood looks different.
And these buildings all look pretty shady...

Where are we heading, Xiao Long?
The Nationless Quarter.
Yokohama Chinatown

Nation-less Quarter?!

What's the matter, Kakeru?!

ガチ SHIVER

ガチ SHIVER

We need to get out of here!

But why? Kaito must be...

Look, we're in danger!

ニヤ
SMIRK
ニヤ
SMIRK
SMIRK
What are you little kids doing in a place like this?
Think they're here to give us some money?!
This is what I was afraid of!
Look, aneko-kun, here's even a irl with hem!

S-See? This is why I wanted to leave!
It's a desolate district in the corner of Yokohama.
Like the name says, it's a place where all languages and cultures mix together.
A lawless neighborhood full of robberies, rapes, and murders. Anything goes here!
Save us the exposition, kid.
SHOVE!!
Oww!
You're pretty cute, sweetheart. What's your name?
Whoa!
I take that back, you're *mega* cute!
Are you a model or something?
Let us show you a good time, baby.

Knock it off!

PUSH

But something tells me... You won't take orders from me... Ha...Ha...

GLARE

Well, Ayano clearly doesn't want to hang out with you, so we'll just be leaving...

C'mon, I know you wanna!
GRAB
Oww, no!
CRACKLE
Stop that or else...
DASH
CRACK
CRACKLE
ZZAP

BWOOOOM

Wha... What was that?!
Flames...?
COUGH
COUGH

Kaito!
DMMM
....

Kaito!

Hey! Looks like you guys made it out all right, too!

Didn't I warn you about this?

Stop picking fights and extorting outsiders!

He's a firestarter.

He can create flames out of thin air with his mind.

Yes, we found him! This is the Kakeru that Jôi told us to find!

Uh... Hi.

That's me, I guess.

....

……

Feh.

Looks like Jôi's losing his edge, to me.

Our future depends on this little ***pussy willow?***

Kaito! You have to believe in Jôi's words!

We have to pool our strength from now on! We'll need your help more than ever!

……

Go home.
Jôi and y'all can still manage against the Farmers.
I've got a place to return to.
I've got my friends to protect here.

And don't come back after me.
Got that?

Oh no no, it doesn't bother me.
It's only the truth.
I think he's a good guy, at heart.
He obviously cares about his friends.
But it doesn't look like he'll come with us.
No, it doesn't.
Well, that just won't do!
Even Kaito will be in danger by himself!
Eventually, the Farmers are going to catch him or kill him!

B-But his powers are so strong. How could they ever beat him...?
The Farmers aren't our only enemies.

......

BWOOOM

Flames just bursting out of nowhere...

That sure was astonishing.

ぐしゃ ぐしゃ

SCRUNCH

SCRUNCH

Oh God, oh God, oh God! Now there's a guy who makes fires!

I get the feeling that I'm ***never*** going to work myself out of this mess now...!

What did they call him? Fire-what...?

This is just crazy!

UNNNG

中華街

Whew... Finally out of the Nationless Quarter.
MURMUR
ガヤ
MURMUR
ガヤ

I figured I would spend my entire vacation playing computer games, and look where I am now.
関帝廟道
30

Though, I guess I could look at it like this: Now I get to enjoy that unreality I've always wanted.
SCRITCH
ぽり
SCRATCH
ぽり
The problem is, this might be just a bit *too* unreal...

Now... How can I kill some time?
And how long is this going to take Ayano?

......
H... Huh...?
TURN

What?
What's going on?!

ガラッ
SHOVE

Wha...?

ガチャ
SHOVE

No...

Someone... Anyone!
Is there anyone here?!

Someone, answer me!

CLUNK

Huh?

There's someone!

Thank goodness...
DASH
I knew it wasn't ESP!!

Um... Excuse me!

Huff, huff... I need to ask you a question...
Huff
Huff
Huff

All of a sudden, everyone disappeared.
Is there some sort of event happening around here?
Like, a parade, or...

......
GIGGLE
Event?
Yes... There sure is.
RISE
Ah... so there *is!* What kind of...

It's a battle to the death...
LURCH

Between psychics.

Uh...

W... What's going on...?!

My name is Maya. Shall we begin?

My new psychic friend.

CASE 3 – Maya

POP

My name is Maya.

LICK

Shall we begin?

My new psychic friend.

LURCH
Mrahh!
Urrrg!
Aaahh!
DASH
Now now, don't bother running...
TOSS
Not that I have a problem with being teased.
ROLL
FWSHH
BZZZZ

W- What's *with* her?!
I think she's crazy!

Huff.
Huff.

日曜·休日の
4月~9月は
13 − 18
10月~3月は
13 − 17
Okay... I think I've run far enough...

SLURCH
?
What's that feeling?

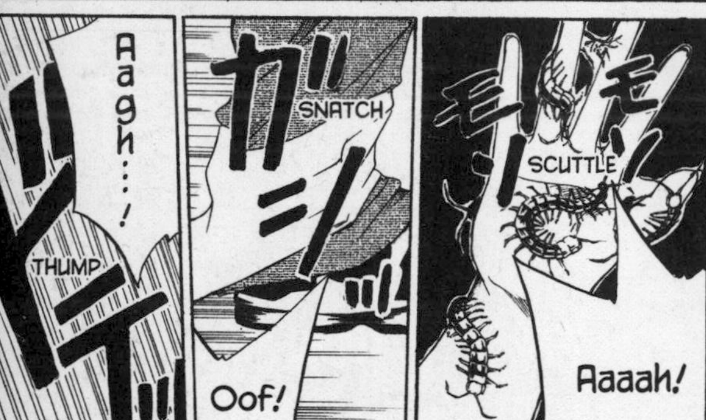
SCUTTLE
Aaaah!
SNATCH
Oof!
THUMP
Aagh...!

Found you.

Didn't I tell you it was pointless to run?
Sheesh... You're just wasting my time...
W- What's going on here?!
Who the heck *are* you, anyway?!
I'm a psychic, obviously.
But I can't tell you what I've done...
You don't really think a psychic gives away her secret powers, do you?
It would be like telling you my weakness.

But *I'm* not a psychic!
Liar.
I've been watching you.
What better proof than that you were with Ayano and her friends?
And even if I *am* wrong...
I'll kill you anyway.
We can't have people learning about us.

N...No fair...!
Well? Shall we get started?
It's not often two psychics get the chance to fight each other.
It's true, I swear!
I have nothing to do with you people!
All right, kid, I've had enough of you.
You want me to bust your skull in right here and now?
Or do you want to be like the people in the neighbor-hood,
And get turned into a zombie?

DODGE
フラッ
Damn!
Ah...
ダッ
DASH
N-Noooo!
Why...
Why isn't there anyone around?!

Huff
huff
huff
What's going on here?!
Have I been trapped...in some other dimension or something?!

Or did she really turn everyone around into zombies?!
Just so she could play this *game* with me?!

That's just too crazy... It's totally insane!

BA-BOOM

Now, let's have some fun.

This psychic death-match should be good.

ROAHHH

DOOM

GLARE

GRAB
All right, then.
You asked for it, you got it.
I'll show you my psychic powers.
......!!

I should have expected this from a wild-type psychic.
PASHHH
You're not too bad at this after all.
Finally in the mood for some fun?

I hate to tell you this,

But your powers will never beat me.

TWITCH

......

What... did you just say...?

Or you'll *die.*

Wha...

Who *are* you...?

Shall I tell you what your powers are?
You claimed to have turned the townspeople into zombies, but that was a lie.

There are no zombies here at all.
And the people in town are perfectly fine... right?
You didn't trap me in some alternate dimension, either.

Yours are the powers of "illusion."
You're simply showing me those sights and nothing else.

......
Correct.
Or is it? How do you know?
Do you have any proof?

TSK TSK
チッ チッ
Just a simple explana-tion.

The way you walked.
When I ran away, it looked like you were weaving and dodging something as you followed me.

I was running and screaming, so the people around me jumped out of the way, but you had to walk around them, didn't you?

In other words...
There are people all around me at this very second. I just can't see them!

But I had also been wondering about some *other* things...
POINT
Like, why were all the people gone, but not the animals?

All it shows is a perfectly peaceful neighborhood sidewalk.

Are you kid-ding?

No psychic would reveal his powers to an enemy.

It's working!
She's totally falling for it!

A total last-minute desperate bluff, and it's working like gangbusters...
REACH
Any closer, and you'll be turned to a crisp.
Crisp...? Fire... Just like Kaito.
She's thinking it over!
No, it could be some sort of electrical attack, too.

All according to plan!
Geh heh heh

Too bad for you, I can keep Ayano and Xiao Long safe on my own.
Both of them?
On your own?
You seem to have quite a lot of confidence in your powers.
SHHH

You bet.
I don't know what you're after, but you'll never lay a finger on them.

......
I must admit, I'm surprised that someone as powerful as you even exists.

It's still working!
Keep laying it on, Kakeru!
SQUEEZE

If I intimi-date her enough...
So why don't you save yourself the trouble and give up now?

Go on.
I'll even let you leave unscathed.
Go on, then!
Please! Just leave me alone!
Or else...

Sounds fun.
Let's do this psychic battle!
HEH
......
Huh?
D... Do you have any idea the danger you're in?
I know what your powers are, too!
Your back's against the wall!
I even told you that your powers would never beat me!

I've always wanted a real survival challenge.

True, my powers are only illusions, but that's not all they do.

Which I'm sure you'll discover once we get started.

LURCH

LURCH

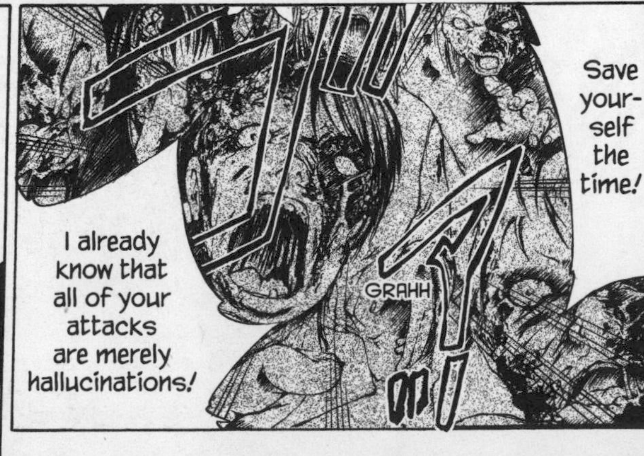

SQUIRT
CHOMP
SQUIRT
CHOMP

They're just illusions...
They can't harm me...

Yeoww-www!
MUNCH
MUNCH

You silly boy.
Illusions can still hurt you.

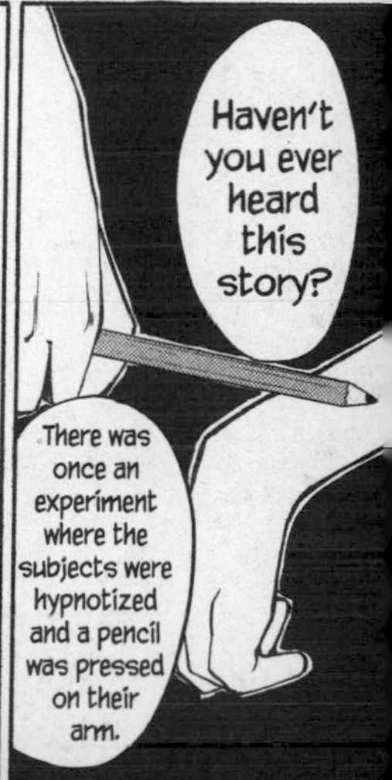
Haven't you ever heard this story?
There was once an experiment where the subjects were hypnotized and a pencil was pressed on their arm.

But they were told it was actually a red-hot poker instead.
And what do you think happened?
They screamed as if actually burned with a poker.

Some of them even developed burn scars on their arms afterward.

Hallucination or not, the pain your brain feels is still real.
Can you stand the pain of having your limbs ripped off?
Oh, crap...
Help!
I'm going to die...
RIP
RIP
RIP
Bye-bye.
Aaaaaugh!
BOOOM
CRACK

Huh?
KRISHHK

BWOOOOOSH

The water tank...?

Aaaaahh!

BLOOSH

WSHHHH

FLOP

FLOP

So, is *that* what you do?
It startled me so much, I released my powers.
You idiot! How did the tank get broken?!
I-I'm sorry, sir! I was only clean-ing like usual...
A cleaning mistake? So it *wasn't* broken by his powers?
He just... got lucky...?
Kakeru Hase...
You could be more fun than you seem.
Sigh. My clothes are soaked. This sucks.
I'll go home...
Guess I'll leave the rest to Shô...

So the water tank breaks out of nowhere and saves me...
Guess I got out by the skin of my teeth once again...
First I need to tell Ayano about this...
Huff
huff
huff
There she is!
Hey, Ayano!
Huff
Ayano!
huff
Good... You're safe, too.
You're not gonna believe this!
I ran into this girl named Maya who's chasing after you guys!
And there might be more psychics around aside from her!
We need to get mov-ing...
SLIP

FWUMP

Huh...? A...

A... Aya... no...?

Xiao Long!
Who are... you...?
What, is this "The End" already?
You guys make a weak audience.

Ayano... Xiao Long...
Sigh... Talk about a disappointment...
My name is Shô... Are you going to be worth a bit more fun than those two?
HUFF
What... *happened* here?!
HUFF

CASE 4 – Shô

Psycho Busters

Kakeru...

huff

huff

R... Run...

I...

I can't do that...

Of course you can't...

Anyone who ran in this situation would be chicken beyond words.

Huh...

Aaagh!

When did you get behind me?!

Those two pipsqueaks were barely worth my time.

BFOOM
Damn!
I know those powers...

Kaito!
Kaito... kun.
Just call me Kaito. We're the same age.
Now take these two out of here, pussy willow.
Huh? But I...
Why would you stick around here?
Uh...
Are you going to be of any use?

……
Long time no see, Kaito.

Shô...
What the hell are you doing here?

Pretty simple, really. I was ordered to capture Jôi.
Capture Jôi-kun...?
Why, you know where he is?

Can't say I do.
Speaking of which...

When did you get those powers?
I don't remember you having psychokinesis.
And the agility to be able to float in midair like that...You'd need a lot of power.
When did I get it...?
You really can't figure that out? It's what the Greenhouse is for.
Drugs, then...
You got it.
We cultivated types aren't like you wild types. We need fertilizer.
Drugs? Cultivated types...?
What in the world is he talking about?

So anyways, you really don't know where Jôi is?
You and I go way back. I'll let you go free if you tell me.

Gosh...
What a generous offer...

But first we've got a little score to settle! I owe you for what you did to Ayano and Xiao Long!
BURRRN
Hah!
This should be good! Let's see what you got, Human Lighter!

SWISH
THUD
THUD
Look out, Kaito!

I'll burn you to a crisp!

FWOOOM

Agh...!
BOOOM
CRSHH
A surprise blast from behind, huh?!
W...

Wow!
Kaito is powerful!
His flames can instantly melt steel knives,
and he wields them so precisely...

!?

BWOOOM

Kaito's abilities are far stronger than anything I've seen so far!

Damn... Sur-rounded!
OOOOO
Can't have you hopping around in midair.

SMIRK

Kaito, get away!

Now there's no escape for you.

Sorry, babe. ♥
FLICK
STAB

Impossible...

How did you get... behind me...?!

TWITCH

You fool!
My power is "teleportation"!
I can't believe you actually fell for that! What a loser!
......
Tele-portation...?
......!!
Of course! He wasn't floating with psy-chokinesis.
He was repeatedly teleport-ing into the same spot in midair!
Now, who should I ask for Jôi's loca-tion?
Ah, of course.
Wasn't there one more person here?
Huh...?
FLICK

Do *you* know where he is?
LICK
If you're hiding the answer from me, I'm just going to have to torture it out of you.
BA-BUMP
BA-BUMP
I'm... the only one left...
Just me...
I have to handle this on my own!

S... Stay back!
Hmm?
Stay back, or else...
I'll activate my powers!
......
Are you sure you want that?!
You'll go down the same way that Maya girl did!
PICK
PICK
I know just the trick...
POINT
I'll bring down a meteorite on your head!

Are you done yet?
GRAB
Huh...
TUG
Ah...
POP
Aaaah!

DROP
Ah...

That's funny.
I thought you said you were going to crush me!

What?
Aren't you going to use your powers?

Aaahhh!

Ha ha ha! That was funny!
K... Kake... ru...

THUD
Unggh...

Huff
Huff
That was... close...
If that pussy willow hadn't shouted when he did, I'd be dead now...
Huff
Huff
Huff
KCHAK
Huff
Next we'll try two meters off the ground.
THUD
But now...
I won't be able to catch Sho with these stab wounds, while he zips around.
And pussy willow's gonna die soon...
Gwaaah!
THUD

Try three meters!

POP

Given up on beating me yet? Feel like talking?
Huff
Huff

GLANCE

Okay then, guess we'll try four meters now!
GRAB

W-What's going on?
What the hell is he thinking?!

Just kidding! It's actually ten. ♥
BAM
I'm getting bored and I want to ask someone else.
Kakeru!
Adios.
DROP

……
What–?
The...
Hell?
When did you do that?!
SQUEEZE

That was pointless!
I'll just drop you from an even higher spot!

SHHHH

Why can't I teleport to another location?!

Just as I thought...

Wh...

You've got a laundry rope around your foot?!
STRETCH

Your powers also teleport everything that's physically connected to you...
Otherwise your clothes wouldn't teleport with you.

Whaaat?!

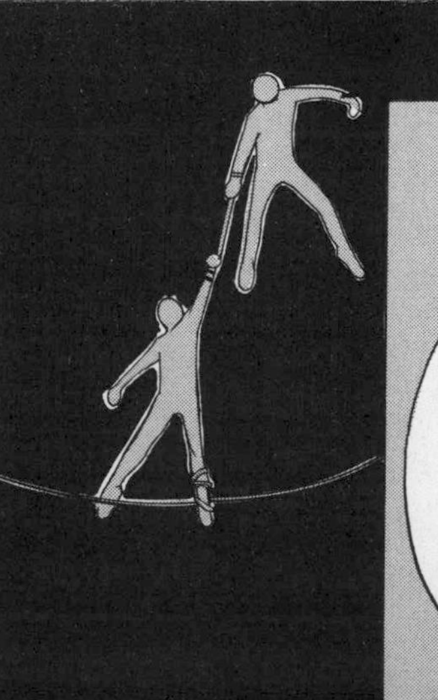

The rope around my foot is connected to these buildings... and even the ground.
But there has to be a limit to the size of what you can teleport.

It doesn't look like you can teleport all of that with you.

And what of it?
What more can you possibly do?
I can use my knife to cut that belt, and that's the end of it!
......

Kaitoooo!

Pussy Willow...?
LURCH

You've still got enough left in you...
For one big blast, right?

Are you kidding...?

You don't think I'm that wussy, do you?
Huff
Huff huff
I'm hurt, so don't complain if my aim is a bit off!
Just make sure you're ready for it!
I like that attitude!
NOD
W-Wait! Let's talk this over!
Like, Love and Peace, right?

I guess you better pray to the god of rock 'n' roll, then!
Aaaagh!
The belt's...
FZZZZ
Snapping...
RIP
GWOOOM
Damn!
LURCH
He got away...
I... did it...
Kakeru!

THUD

......

Sheesh...

Crazy kid.

Bet he never even considered that this could have killed him...

Then again, we *do* have Xiao Long...

But maybe Jôi was right, after all. Maybe there *is* something to him.

I could have died if he hadn't warned me when he did.

Thanks, Kakeru.

What's that?
I hear voices...

Hmm?
It's warm...

Oh...

Kakeru!
SQUEEZE

Uh...
Aya... no...
I'm so glad you're safe... So glad...

BA-BUMP
A-Are you okay?
BA-BUMP
Xiao Long healed me!
Sorry...
It all worked out, though...
You have no idea how worried I was!
PUSH
Huh?
Pshh. Fine...
Huh?! Then, you mean...
Well, Kaito? Kakeru kept us safe, didn't he?
Jôi's words were correct! Our future depends on Kakeru!
Um... Actually, I don't know...
Yeah, I'll work with you guys for the time being.
T-This is all too sudden...
Yayyy! Now we're all together!

But don't get the wrong idea. I'm just more worried for your sake than the guys here.

If it gets you to come with us, then it's enough for me!

And with Kakeru on our side, we're unstoppable!

What?! I'm included in all of this?!

Of course! We're a team, aren't we?!

Uh, but...I'm not a psychic...

It'll be good working with you.

It...It *will* be...?

A Note from the Creator

Nice to meet you. I'm Akinari Nao. This is my first manga volume. This was only possible with the help of the author, Aoki-sensei, the artist who drew the illustrations in his original novels, Ayamine-sensei, my editor and staff, friends and family, and, of course, everyone who took the time to read this book.

I'll do my best.

STAFF: Yûya Aoki
Akinari Nao

Tatsu Nakajima
Naoto Shinoda
Kiyomizu
Takuya Suzuki (Help)

SPECIAL THANKS:
Keitarô Yanagibashi

Staff Introduction

Special Thanks Illustration

Special Thanks Illustration

Special Thanks Illustration

My editor always tells me to make it "more sexy" when we discuss the next chapter. I'm sorry... This is the best I can do.

Special Thanks Illustration

This is a rough illustration for the Magazine Special calendar. I was told it would be for the October page, so I tried to give it that sort of feeling.

Translation Notes

Japanese is a tricky language for most Westerners, and translation is often more an art than a science. For your edification and reading pleasure, here are notes on some of the places where we could have gone in a different direction, or where a Japanese cultural reference is used.

Branch office, page 13

It's not uncommon in Japan for employees of large companies that have multiple offices around the country to be transferred to another location for an extended period, especially if they are in management. In this case, Kakeru's father is currently on such an assignment.

Nanan, page 14

This is a parody of the popular *shôjo* manga *Nana* by Ai Yazawa. Apparently, Kakeru is too embarrassed to ask his sisters if he can borrow their manga when they're around!

High school uniform porno, page 14

Because virtually every high school in Japan has mandatory uniform rules, the image of school girls in uniform is virtually synonymous with nubile, teenage adolescence. Therefore it is a very common sexual fetish for Japanese men.

Ofuda, page 30

Ofuda are small Shinto talismans, usually strips of paper, designed to bring good luck to the bearer. In fictional and magical settings, these charms typically have spells written on them by a priest or sorcerer and are said to combat evil spirits or *oni*, by either sealing them or driving them away.

Astral projection, page 38

When Kakeru asks for the kanji for "astral projection," he wants to know the Chinese characters that make up the meaning of the word. Literally translated, the kanji for *yûtai-ridatsu* (astral projection) mean "ghost-body-separation," so when he hears "ghost," he assumes she *is* a ghost after all.

Yi, er, san, etc., page 46

The list of words Xiao Long strings together are the Mandarin Chinese numbers from one to ten.

Qigong, page 51

Qigong is a system of breathing exercises taught either as a method of health maintenance or with Chinese martial arts. While Xiao Long's uses of *qigong* are certainly highly fictionalized, there are some who believe *qigong* holds spiritual and mystical benefits.

Guns, page 53

While having a loaded gun pointed at your head would make *anyone* nervous, Kakeru is especially shocked. His disbelief comes from the fact that handguns are illegal for Japanese citizens to own due to very strict weapon control laws. Simply encountering a real firearm in any manner would be nearly unthinkable to a modern Japanese citizen.

Yokohama, page 94

Yokohama is known for having one of the largest Chinatowns in the world and by far the largest in Japan. Though its actual Chinese population is only a few thousand, there are over two hundred Chinese restaurants in the area.

Firestarter, page 113

Kakeru can't remember the name of Kaito's power because the word is foreign to him. In this case, they are using an approximation of the English "firestarter" that sounds like *faiâsutâtâ*.

Shô, page 161

Though it's difficult to represent in translation, Shô uses a lot of English words in his speech. Perhaps this facet of his flashy character is related to the fact that his name sounds like the word "show."

Kaito, page 167

Kaito tells Kakeru not to call him "Kaito-kun" but just "Kaito." The act of dropping any honorific from a name is called *yobisute* in Japanese. While the use of *-kun* is often relegated to people who are younger or subordinate to the speaker, in the case of two teenage boys who are the same age, it actually creates a distance, perhaps of unfamiliarity or cautious respect between them. Kaito is clearly more comfortable with Kakeru informally calling him "Kaito."

Preview of Volume 2

We're pleased to present you with a preview of volume 2. Please check our website (www.delreymanga.com) to see when this volume will be available in English. For now you'll have to make do with Japanese!

いやあぁあ——!!!

あや‥の‥‥
逃げ‥‥
なんで‥
なんでよ
カケル‥!!
どうしてよぉ!!!
ははっ
とんだ騎士気取り
だな

まぁ オレは『カテゴリ0』を倒せればそれでいいんだけど
猛丸・・・・
これで最後だ!!

PUMPKIN SCISSORS

RYOUTARO IWANAGA

AFTER THE WAR. BEFORE THE PEACE.

Years of bitter war have devestated the Empire. Disease and privation ravage the land. Maurading bandits prey on the innocent.

To aid reconstruction, the Empire has formed Imperial Army State Section III, a.k.a. the Pumpkin Scissors, an elite unit dedicated to protecting the people.

They are the last best hope hope for a beleaguered nation. But will they be enough?

Special extras in each volume! Read them all!

VISIT WWW.DELREYMANGA.COM TO:

- Read sample pages
- View release date calendars for upcoming volumes
- Sign up for Del Rey's free manga e-newsletter
- Find out the latest about new Del Rey Manga series

RATING OT AGES 16+

TOMARE!

[STOP!]

You're going the wrong way!

Manga is a completely different type of reading experience.

To start at the *beginning* go to the *end*!

That's right! Authentic manga is read the traditional Japanese way—from right to left, exactly the *opposite* of how American books are read. It's easy to follow: Just go to the other end of the book, and read each page—and each panel—from right side to left side, starting at the top right. Now you're experiencing manga as it was meant to be.